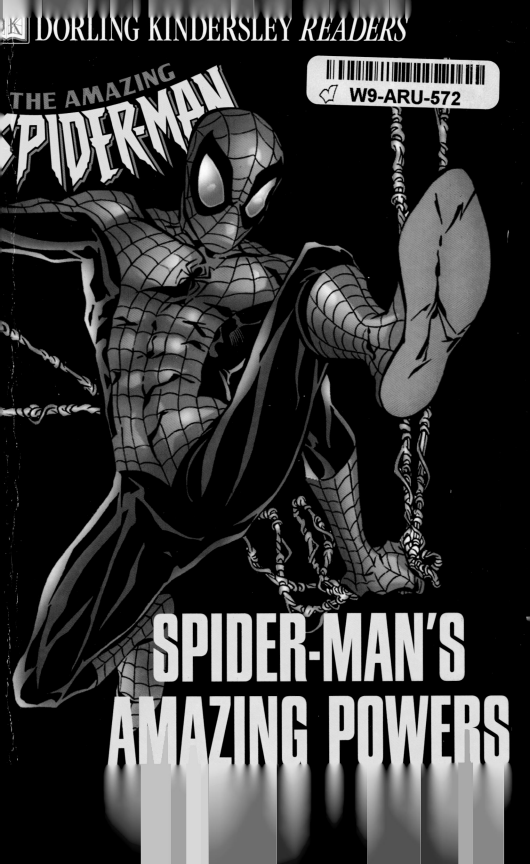

THE AMAZING
SPIDER-MAN

SPIDER-MAN'S AMAZING POWERS

▣K DORLING KINDERSLEY *READERS*

Level 2

Dinosaur Dinners
Firefighter!
Bugs! Bugs! Bugs!
Slinky, Scaly Snakes!
Animal Hospital
The Little Ballerina
Munching, Crunching, Sniffing
  and Snooping
The Secret Life of Trees
Winking, Blinking, Wiggling,
  and Waggling

Astronaut: Living in Space
Twisters!
Holiday! Celebration Days
  around the World
The Story of Pocahontas
Horse Show
Survivors: The Night the Titanic
  Sank
Eruption! The Story of Volcanoes
LEGO: Castle Under Attack!
LEGO: Rocket Rescue

Level 3

Spacebusters
Beastly Tales
Shark Attack!
Titanic
Invaders from Outer Space
Movie Magic
Plants Bite Back!
Time Traveler
Bermuda Triangle

Tiger Tales
Aladdin
Heidi
Zeppelin: The Age of the Airship
Spies
Terror on the Amazon
Disasters at Sea
The Story of Anne Frank
LEGO: Mission to the Arctic

Level 4

Days of the Knights
Volcanoes
Secrets of the Mummies
Pirates!
Horse Heroes
Trojan Horse
Micro Monsters
Going for Gold!
Extreme Machines
Flying Ace: The Story of
  Amelia Earhart
Robin Hood
Black Beauty
Free at Last! The Story of
  Martin Luther King, Jr.
Joan of Arc
Spooky Spinechillers

Welcome to The Globe! The Story
  of Shakespeare's Theatre
Antarctic Adventure
Space Station
Atlantis
Dinosaur Detectives
Danger on the Mountain: Scaling
  the World's Highest Peaks
LEGO: Race for Survival
WCW: Going for Goldberg
WCW: Feel the Sting!
WCW: Fit for the Title
WCW: Finishing Moves
The Story of the X-Men: How it
  all Began
Creating the X-Men: How Comic
  Books Come to Life

A Note to Parents and Teachers

Dorling Kindersley Readers is a compelling program for beginning readers, designed in conjunction with leading literacy experts.

Superb full-color photographs combine with engaging, easy-to-read text to offer a fresh approach to each subject in the series. Each Dorling Kindersley Reader is guaranteed to capture a child's interest, while developing his or her reading skills, general knowledge, and love of reading.

The four levels of Dorling Kindersley Readers are aimed at different reading abilities, enabling you to choose the books that are exactly right for your child:

Level 1 – Beginning to read
Level 2 – Beginning to read alone
Level 3 – Reading alone
Level 4 – Proficient readers

The "normal" age at which a child begins to read can be anywhere from three to eight years old, so these levels are intended only as a general guideline.

No matter which level you select, you can be sure that you are helping your child learn to read, then read to learn!

Dorling  Kindersley

LONDON, NEW YORK, SYDNEY, DELHI, PARIS,
MUNICH, and JOHANNESBURG

Art Director Cathy Tincknell
Publishing Manager Cynthia O'Neill
DTP Designer Jill Bunyan
Production Nicola Torode

Produced by Shoreline Publishing Group
Editorial Director James Buckley, Jr.
Art Director Thomas J. Carling,
Carling Design Inc.

First American Edition, 2001
Published in the United States by
DK Publishing, Inc.
95 Madison Ave., New York, NY 10016

01 02 03 04 05 10 9 8 7 6 5 4 3 2

Library of Congress Cataloging-in-Publication Data
Buckley, James Jr.
Spider-Man's amazing powers / by James Buckley, Jr.--
1st American ed.
p. cm. -- (DK Readers)
Summary: Describes Spider-Man's super powers, from web-slinging
and wall-crawling to the mysterious "spider-sense."
ISBN 0-7894-7922-2 (lib. bdg. : alk. paper) --
ISBN 0-7894-7923-0 (pbk.)
[1. Heroes--Fiction.] I. Title: Spider-Man's amazing powers. II. Title.
III. Dorling Kindersley readers.
PZ.T233 Swk 2001
[E]--dc21
2001017402

Color reproduction by MDP
Printed and bound in China by L. Rex

Photography and illustration credits:
t=top, b=below, l=left, r=right, c=center,
**All Spider-Man and other character illustrations
courtesy Marvel Enterprises, Inc.**
Dorling Kindersley picture collection: 4cl, 6bl, 8b, 10tl, 12bl, 13tr,
14tl, 16bl, 17tr, 23rt, 24tl,
26bl, 30tl, 34cl, 36tl, 45tr, 46tl;
Corbis: 4bl, 8tl, 15br, 19br, 35bl, 41t, 41b, 47cr.

see our complete
catalog at
www.dk.com

Contents

SPIDER-MAN'S
AMAZING POWERS

Written by James Buckley, Jr.

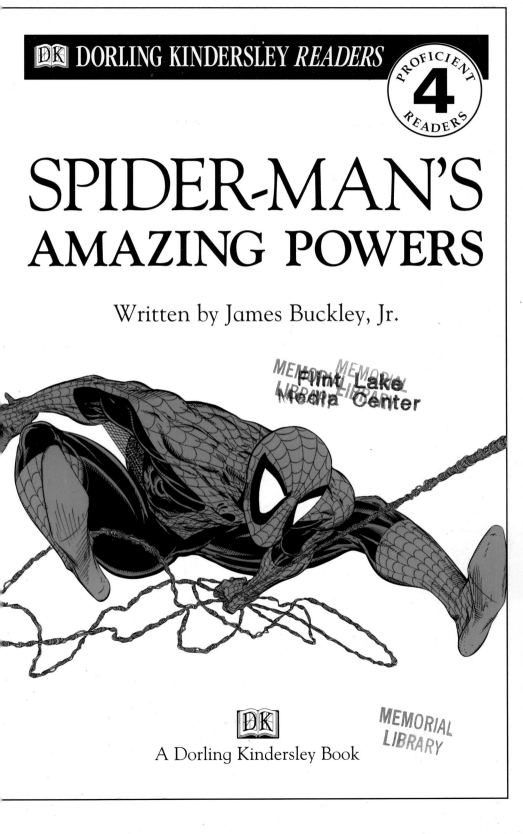

DK

A Dorling Kindersley Book

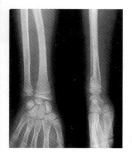

Power bite

The most important moment in Peter Parker's life happened by surprise. He was a high school student at a science fair. Passing through an exhibit on radioactivity, he felt a sharp pain in his hand.

Peter looked down to see that a spider had bitten him!

Man, that hurts, Peter thought. What he didn't know was that the spider bite would change the course of his life.

Why? Because that spider had been affected by a experiment at the science fair. Powerful rays had changed the spider, giving its bite a unique and strange effect. The person it bit received incredible powers…the powers of a spider.

Soon Peter noticed some odd things happening to him. He could stick to walls, and he had developed amazing strength.

IN AGONY, THE DYING SPIDER SPUN ABOUT-- WAFTING THROUGH THE AIR, AND LANDING ON THE UNSUSPECTING HIGHSCHOOLER...

OW!

This spider bite turned plain old Peter Parker into the web-swinging super hero Spider-Man!

He had an unusual tingling "spider-sense." He could climb anything, just like a spider.

Peter had been changed from an everyday high school student into the amazing Spider-Man!

Don't call them bugs
Spiders should not be called insects or bugs. All spiders are arachnids [ah-RACK-nids], a special family of animals.

5

Spider-Man's distinctive, skin-tight, red-and-blue costume features a spider web design and a mask to conceal his real identity.

Birth of Spidey Spider-Man first appeared in Amazing Fantasy #15 in 1963. He was created by Stan Lee, a famous comic-book writer and editor.

Over the years, Marvel Comics, a company located in New York City, has created many great super heroes, including the X-Men, the Fantastic Four, the Avengers, and more.

But perhaps the most popular is Spider-Man. He has the most unique set of powers of them all.

To the gifts the spider had given him, Peter added special web-shooters that he has put to thousands of uses. He has traveled the earth and the universe defending the innocent and rescuing people in trouble.

But while he has thrilled his fans with his great feats of strength and courage, "Spidey," as he's also called, is a joke-telling, regular guy from New York City...who just happens to be able to swing from buildings, lift buses, and stick to walls and ceilings!

In this book, read all the secret details of each of Spider-Man's special powers, learn how they relate to real spiders, and learn how he uses his powers to help others.

Covering Spider-Man
Spidey stars in several Marvel monthly titles.

Home-field advantage
The 1,453-foot Empire State Building is one of the buildings Spidey uses to swing around.

Web building
These drawings show how a spider builds a web. It begins with a frame and then adds strands inside the frame.

Wonderful webs

What's the first thing you think of when you picture a spider? Eww, gross, right? Okay, well what's the second thing? That's right...webs.

Spiders spin webs as places to live and as traps to capture their prey. When Peter Parker became Spider-Man, he knew that he would need the spider's ability to spin webs. But the spider's bite had not given him any way to produce the super-strong silk threads that spiders use to make webs.

So Peter turned to chemistry. Always a great science student himself, Peter created a secret liquid formula that he used to form Spider-Man's webs.

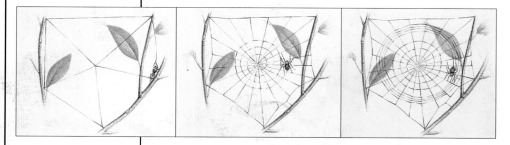

With this formula, he could shoot webs of all shapes and sizes to use in different ways.

Spidey's costume is covered with a web design.

He has web-shooters on both wrists.

Swinging from one web, Spider-Man shoots out another strand in front of him. Doing this over and over lets him swing through the city.

9

Geronimo!
Spiders use
their webbing
to swing from
place to place
or as a sort of
parachute shot
out behind
them.

But how does Spider-Man shoot
his webs? Spiders have a special
body part on their abdomen
[AB-duh-men], or stomach,
that shoots out a thin strand of silk
which they use to spin webs.

Spider-Man created special
devices that he wears around each
wrist. A trigger button rests in the
palm of each hand.

**It's all in
the wrist**
The web fluid is
contained in
rectangular
cartridges that
Spider-Man
snaps into place
in the cuffs, as
shown here.

By pushing down on the
trigger with his middle two fingers,
he shoots out a strand of webbing.

The web fluid zaps out of an
opening in the wrist device and
instantly turns into extremely strong
strands of webbing.

10

Some estimates say that strands of Spidey's webbing are strong enough to support 10 tons per square inch. That comes in handy when Spider-Man is trying to stop a massive object from falling onto himself or others.

Battery compartmant

Spinneret nozzle

Trigger

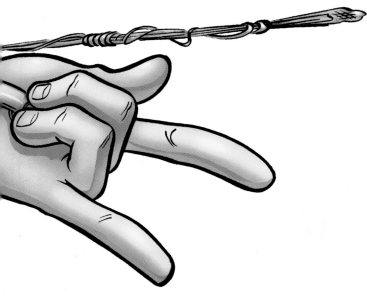

Spiders' bodies make web silk, so it's hard for them to run out. But Spidey can run out of web fluid, like a car can run out of gas.

Inside the web-shooter
Here's a close-up of the inside of the web-shooter. The fluid shoots out through the spinneret nozzle when Spidey presses the palm trigger.

Extra formula
Spider-Man wears a special belt to carry his extra cartridges of web fluid. Also, the center of the belt is an intense flashlight.

Spiders can move from place to place by walking, swinging, or gliding along web strands that they shoot out.

Spider-Man does the same thing. When he wants to go somewhere, he shoots a web to the nearest tall building and starts swinging like Tarzan in the jungle. He swings as far as he can on one strand, then shoots out another one ahead of him, grabbing onto it to continue his swing. He can move through New York City like a monkey, swinging and jumping from place to place high above the city streets.

Look out below
Spider-Man can form his webbing into many shapes, including this parachute.

Tarzan
Tarzan was a character created by Edgar Rice Burroughs for novels, films, and comics.

This is harder to do in wide, flat country than it is in the middle of the big city. But Spider-Man is creative when he has to be. Sometimes he'll hitch a ride on top of a train or a big truck to get where he's going.

Spider-Man and his webbing are even strong enough to hook onto low-flying airplanes or helicopters for a very quick trip.

Unstuck
Why don't spiders stick to their own webs? Because their legs have a special anti-stick covering, and they only touch the web with the tips of their "feet."

Spider-Man combines great gymnastic ability with his incredible web strands to go flying high over the city.

Pack it up
To carry the clothes that he needs to wear as Peter Parker, Spider-Man often makes a backpack out of webbing.

Gotcha!
When made into a net, Spider-Man's web is strong enough to catch a person falling from a great height.

Spider-Man's strong webbing comes in handy in other ways. Along with being strong enough to support him (and anyone else he might be carrying), the webbing can stop vehicles from fleeing. Like a very long, extra-stretchy rubber band, the webbing snatches the back of the car and then – *boing* – pulls it backward.

If the Green Goblin, one of Spidey's longtime enemies, is flying away, Spider-Man can zap webbing onto the bat-shaped flying machine the Goblin uses and haul him back in like a fish on a line.

Or if he's being chased, Spidey can shoot a strand of webbing onto a large object and, using his spider-strength, pull down the whole thing down on top of his pursuers.

Spider-Man's webbing is so strong that this enormous iron safe can dangle safely from one thin strand.

Old spiders
The oldest spider fossils date back 380 million years. Today, science has identified more than 35,000 types of spiders.

Spooky webs
Old spider webs that remain behind after a spider has left often gather dust. These are called cobwebs.

He can also use the webbing to snatch away weapons.

Spider-Man also has used webbing to create a man-sized dummy to fool his enemies.

15

All wrapped up
Using his webbing as wrapping paper, Spidey made these villains into a Christmas present.

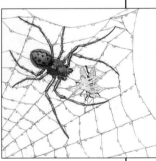

Insect soup
Spiders don't eat their prey. They dissolve the insect with venom and then suck it in with their strawlike mouth.

The secret chemical makeup of Spider-Man's webbing lets it dissolve after about two hours. Real spiders' webbing takes much longer to dissolve, for good reason. After spiders have captured a fly or mosquito, they wrap up the unfortunate creature. The web forms a cocoon around the meal until the spider needs it.

Spider-Man does something similar. When he captures criminals in the act, and he can't wait around for the police, he quickly surrounds the felons with sticky, super-strong webbing that they can't break.

Whether his enemies shoot flamethrowers, lightning bolts, or powerful jets of water, Spider-Man's webbing is strong enough to block them all.

After the webbing dissolves, the police take the suspects away. Officers who find a web-covered crook hanging from a lamppost know that Spider-Man is on the job.

Thanks to his own creativity and some ingenious devices, Spider-Man was able to mimic a spider's greatest power, even without help from a radioactive spider bite.

Safe and sound
Many spiders also use their webbing to wrap their eggs in a ball. This keeps the eggs safe until the young spiders are old enough to come out.

Fireproof
Spider-Man's webbing is nearly fireproof. He can form a thick shield with the webbing that can block even the heat of this powerful flamethrower.

Spider hiders
Spiders use their ability to stick upside down to find great hiding places in high, dark corners, keeping them safe from harm.

Wall-crawler

Have you ever looked up at the ceiling and seen a spider hanging there, upside down? Or watched a spider walk up a wall that any other kind of animal would simply fall off?

Spiders have special feet at the end of their eight legs that allow them to grab onto any surface with a tight grip. Since being bitten by the radioactive spider, Spider-Man has the same powerful grip in his fingers and toes.

This "wall-crawling" ability was the first power Peter Parker learned about. While leaving the science fair after he had been bitten, he was nearly hit by a speeding car. To avoid it, he leaped to the side …and stuck to a nearby building!

Soon Peter, as Spider-Man, learned that he could crawl up the sides of a room or a building. He could stick upside down to a ceiling. He could leap to almost anywhere and stick to it, just as a spider grabs onto a wall and hangs there like a painting.

Up and away
Spider-Man doesn't need his costume to cling to walls. Here, Peter Parker sticks to a building.

Sticky feet
Spider's legs have special claws and hundreds of sticky hairs that let them cling to both smooth and rough surfaces.

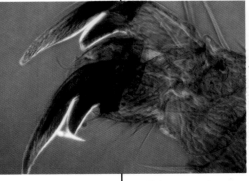

Sticky fingers
To climb the high walls of buildings, Spider-Man simply "walks" on his hands and tiptoes.

Quick change
Sticking to walls makes it easy for Peter Parker to find a quiet place to change into his Spider-Man costume.

Being able to stick like a spider to just about anything has a lot of advantages if you're a super hero like Spider-Man.

For example, Spidey can wait inside a room for villains to enter. Instead of hiding behind the couch or the door or someplace they might easily find him, he can hang onto the ceiling and drop down on top of them before they know what hit them.

Anyone who thinks they can hide from Spider-Man is wrong. With an ability to walk up walls, Spider-Man can get inside any building. He can climb through air vents or go down chimneys.

ONE TH
YOU MUS
WE'VE PRE
ABOUT A
PANELS
TYPE S
SPIDEY W
INTROD
RIGHT

Spider-Man once had to find someone who was hiding on the 50th floor of a high-rise in New York, with armed guards at the door to the room. The man was very surprised when he heard a tap on the window. It was Spider-Man on a stroll...400 feet above the sidewalk!

High-rise
The first high-rise buildings were built late in the 1800s as new techniques for creating steel frames and elevators were developed.

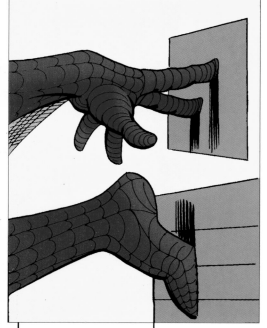

One of Spider-Man's most valuable assets is his CLINGING ABILITY! Like a giant human spider, his hands and feet support him against the pull of gravity as though they have thousands of tiny suction cups!

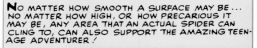

No matter how smooth a surface may be...no matter how high, or how precarious it may be, any area that an actual spider can cling to, can also support the amazing teenage adventurer!

Stick it to me
Spidey's ability to stick to anything rests mostly in his hands and feet, especially in his fingertips. The rest of his body isn't sticky enough to use on walls, but it is sticky enough to hold onto a squirming enemy during a fight.

Spidey's ability to walk on walls has also given him one of his most popular nicknames: "Wall-crawler." Often people will refer to "the wall-crawler" or "that darn wall-crawler." Sometimes people mean the nickname in a nice way...sometimes they don't! Of course, he can do more than crawl up walls...he can even run!

But how does he do these amazing "sticky" tricks? Because the spider's bite changed his body in some mysterious way. Now his hands, the tips of his fingers, his toes, and his feet can form an incredibly tight bond with any surface. The bond can support the weight of his body and often much more than that.

Another good thing about being able to stick to anything is that it makes it much harder to fall. While out on patrol, Spidey has been swinging high above the streets of New York when *click*…suddenly, he runs out of his all-important, top-secret web fluid.

He falls, of course, but thanks to his sticky power, he can grab a hold of something to save himself.

Hanging out
Like Spider-Man, spiders like this one can hang from any surface, including upside down from this plant, by using their sticky feet.

Eight or four?
Spiders can use all eight legs to cling to any surface, while Spider-Man has to depend on just four limbs.

Sssss!
One of Spider-Man's enemies is The Lizard, who was created when scientist Curt Connors drank a secret potion.

Finally, thanks to his sticky fingers, once Spider-Man grabs a hold of something, you're probably not going to get it back from him.

However, this can backfire on Spider-Man. While his spider-strength can help him hold on tightly, and his stickiness will make him stick there forever if wants to, there is a solution for his enemies.

They simply pull down the whole wall – Spider-Man and all. Occasionally, Spidey has found himself flying across a room still attached to a wall panel, a ceiling tile, or a door. The building materials weren't as strong as his grip, so *crrrack!* Off they come.

However, most of the people and things he battles aren't strong enough to overcome his mighty spider-grip.

"I'VE NEVER COME ACROSS ANYTHING THAT CAN ACTUALLY *SEPARATE* ME FROM A SURFACE ONCE I'VE STUCK TO IT--

"-- ALTHOUGH I'VE BEEN IN SOME SITUATIONS WHERE THE SURFACE *BROKE* UNDER THE STRAIN!

One problem he has with this power is that he must be careful never to use it when he's not in his Spider-Man costume. If someone saw Peter Parker climbing along the ceiling at the mall, Spider-Man's secret identity might not be secret for much longer.

Crrrack!
To rip Spider-Man from his perch, super-strong Colossus of the X-Men simply rips down the wall, bringing the super-sticky Spider-Man with it.

Spiders come in all sizes. The smallest are less than one-eighth of an inch across. The largest is the Goliath spider, which is as big as a dinner plate!

Ooof!
Many athletes train by lifting weights. There are also competitions among weightlifters, such as in the Olympics.

Spider-strength

How much do you weigh? How much weight can you lift? Even if you're strong, you probably can't lift much more weight than the number of pounds you weigh. Spiders, however, can lift many times their own body weight.

Spider-Man gained that same ability when he was bitten by the radioactive spider. Spidey can lift hundreds of times his own body weight. It is called having the "proportionate" [pro-PORSH-in-et] strength of a spider. That is, Spider-Man is as strong compared to other humans as a spider is compared to other animals.

Peter Parker is an ordinary-sized guy, not too big and not too small. He weighs only 165 pounds. Next to other super heroes, he's puny.

Spider-Man shows off his amazing strength by lifting these other Marvel super heroes: (left to right) Thing, Hercules, Thor, Sub-Mariner, and Hulk.

The fellow on the ground at right is happy that his friendly neighborhood Spider-Man just happened to be around when this bus was about to fall on him.

Building blocks
All human cells contain a chemical called DNA, which is formed in long, twisting strands like the ones below. DNA forms the code that creates all life. When Peter Parker's DNA was changed by the spider's venom, Peter's body changed, too, giving him his amazing powers.

Spider-Man isn't muscle-bound; he doesn't have gigantic arms or huge legs. Like a spider, he's slender and agile. But the radioactive bite of that spider deeply affected Peter Parker.

How? By changing Peter's genetic structure, turning his ordinary muscles into ones filled with spider-strength.

The spider's venom [VENN-um], or poison, had been affected by the radioactivity. When the spider bit Peter, its venom actually changed Peter's muscles and other body parts.

The bite turned a regular guy into a powerhouse of strength.

Now, for instance, when a helicopter is falling onto some innocent people, instead of watching them get squashed like, well, like a spider, Spidey can catch the chopper before it hits the ground so the people can escape. He also can lift heavy objects from the ground.

Spider-Man has used his spider-strength to lift huge weights many times, before they could smash him or someone else.

Watch out! This spider is called a black widow. It's one of the few spiders in the world whose venom is dangerous to humans. A bite from a black widow is 15 times more deadly than a bite from a rattlesnake.

Barbells
Weightlifters
use a piece of
equipment
called a barbell,
which is an iron
rod that holds
heavy steel
disks at each
end. Extra disks
can be added to
make the
barbell harder
to lift.

The family
Peter Parker
was raised by
his Aunt May.

Spider-strength can also be used to bend or twist materials that normal men couldn't even pick up.

Spidey can toss giant weights at crooks, and he can break out of just about anything they strap him into (even Spider-Man gets caught once in a while). Surround him with heavy iron chains, and he can snap them like they were made of paper.

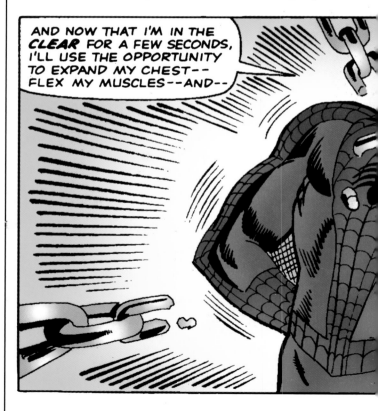

AND NOW THAT I'M IN THE **CLEAR** FOR A FEW SECONDS, I'LL USE THE OPPORTUNITY TO EXPAND MY CHEST-- FLEX MY MUSCLES--AND--

Like his special sticky power, Peter Parker has to be careful about using his spider-strength. When not in costume, he can't go around lifting huge weights or breaking chains. His secret identity helps keep his family and friends safe from Spider-Man's enemies.

Heavy iron chains can't withstand the might of Spider-Man.

Doc Ock
One of Spider-Man's deadliest foes is Doctor Octopus. "Doc Ock" has added four powerful metal arms to his body, which put Spider-Man's strength to the test. Why is he called "Octopus?" Because the octopus, an undersea creature, has eight limbs, too.

--PRESTO!! I FEEL LIKE STEVE REEVES, IN ONE OF THOSE ITALIAN COSTUME MOVIES!

However, spider-strength is very useful when battling enormous enemies like Kingpin, one of Spidey's long-time foes. Kingpin is a mountain of a man whose hands are as big as manhole covers and whose shoulders won't fit through most doors. But thanks to spider-strength, Spider-Man can go toe to toe with the gigantic crook.

Whether he is wrestling the Green Goblin or slugging the Vulture or battling the powerful Venom, Spider-Man's spider-strength is his second-most powerful weapon when it comes to fighting.

What's his most powerful weapon? His imaginative mind and positive outlook. It's no use having enormous strength if you can't think of new and different ways to use it.

Spider-Man's great strength and agility come in handy when battling villains like the Vulture.

Mean green
The Green Goblin is Spider-Man's oldest and greatest foe.

Really bad
Venom is one of Spider-Man's most dangerous enemies. He wears a spiderlike suit that turns him into a super-powered being.

One kind of spider, called the "jumping spider," can make leaps more than 60 times its own body length.

Four times as agile
A spider's eight legs are equally divided, with four on each side of its body. The legs are attached to the abdomen, the second of its two main body parts. The other part is called the cephalothorax.

Catch him if you can

Can a spider dodge a bullet? Probably not. But Spider-Man can, thanks to the agility [ADJ-il-e-tee] and speed the spider's bite gave him. Compared to humans, spiders are much quicker, much more mobile, and thanks to their eight legs, able to move suddenly in all directions.

Watching Spider-Man leap around a room filled with crooks reminds you of a spider dancing around its web.

Of course, a spider isn't slugging crooks in the mouth or dodging knives and bullets. But Spider-Man's agility, like his strength, is proportional to a spider's. That is, he is as agile compared to other humans as a spider is compared to other animals its size. Thanks to this spider power, Spidey can bounce around a room like a human superball.

The incredible Hulk may be stronger than Spider-Man, but Spidey is much quicker.
He uses his agility to stay away from the Hulk's powerful fists.

Look, up in the sky!
Young spiders shoot out short strands of webbing and float, or "balloon," from a high branch to a low one.

In the gym
Gymnasts are the athletes who best combine strength and agility.

Spiders can move quickly in all directions. But can spiders fly? Well, not exactly. But some types of young spiders can sail through the air for short distances, sometimes attached to web strands. Their light weight allows them to glide from place to place, helped by gravity.

Spider-Man can't fly either, but his great leaping ability, along with the use of his web fluid, allows him to travel much farther than a normal person could leap.

A normal person who wore Spider-Man's wrist cuffs still wouldn't be able to swing as well as Spidey. Spidey's extra agility lets him swing freely while using his special web-shooters.

Add that ability to his spider-strength and you'd better be pretty far away from him if you want to avoid getting caught.

Spiderlike agility has kept Spider-Man safe over the years. He uses it, along with spider-sense to get out of trouble.

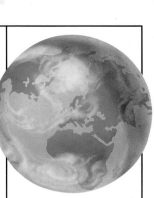

AND NOW, I'LL MAKE A PAIR OF WINGS OUT OF MY WEB FLUID, AND CRASH - DIVE DOWN AND *PULVERIZE* YOU!

Like spiders gliding on their web strands, Spidey can use his webbing to make wings to glide short distances.

Gravity
Why do things fall? Because of the force of gravity [GRAV-ih-tee]. The earth rotates, or spins, causing this "sticky" force that keeps us all anchored to the ground. Without gravity, we'd all fly off into space. Spider-Man spends a lot of his time trying to overcome the power of gravity as he swings from place to place.

Since it reacts to *any* form of danger or menace, I can't be caught by surprise!

"No one—including my own wife—can sneak up on me, or ambush me from behind!"

Is ESP real?
Some people believe that they can predict the future, or that they have special insight into what people are thinking. One form of this is called "extra sensory perception," or ESP.

Tingling feeling

Did you ever get the feeling that you were being watched? Or that something surprising was just about to happen to you?

Whenever Spider-Man is in danger, he gets that feeling… multiplied by 100! Like ESP, his "spider-sense" alerts him when an enemy is getting near, or when someone he knows is in trouble.

Many times, spider-sense has saved Spider-Man from being squashed. It begins with a tiny tingle, a little buzz in the back of his head that slowly gets louder and stronger as danger approaches.

As the buzzing gets stronger, Spider-Man gets more and more alert to trouble from all sides. Just as the danger strikes, Spider-Man can duck, dive, jump, or do whatever it takes to get out of the way. He can sense oncoming missiles or bullets, and he can feel when an enemy is lying in wait for him.

Knowing when something bad is going to happen helps Spider-Man make sure it doesn't happen to him!

Look for waves
In Spider-Man comic books, you can tell when he's getting signals from his amazing spider-sense because these wavy lines appear around his head. They sometimes appear in bright colors, too.

Spiders in real life use something
like spider-sense. Spiders spin webs
to capture their food, such as
insects. When insects land on the
web, spiders can feel the vibrations
along the many strands of silk that
make up each spider's web.
These vibrations are very similar
to the tingling that Spidey feels
when his spider-sense kicks in.

After spinning the web, the
spiders move to one part of it,
often away from the center.
Since all the web strands
connect, if you touch one strand,
all the strands vibrate. Then
they wait for something to get
stuck in the webbing.

When something has touched
or landed on their web, spiders
feel vibrations through their body.
The vibrations might be only a leaf
falling on the web, but other times it
could be something that eats spiders.

Spiders have eight eyes, but don't really use them very much. They have special, very sensitive organs on their legs that tell them when something has landed on the web. These organs also taste, smell, and tell temperature.

Time for lunch
Spiders can eat insects that are larger than they are because the spider's venom paralyzes the prey first.

However, most often, when spiders feel something landing on or moving around on their web, it doesn't mean danger…it means dinner, and the spiders move in for the kill.

Of course, Spider-Man doesn't use his spider-sense to find his dinner; for that, he just uses a menu!

Sniff, sniff
Bloodhounds are dogs with an unusually powerful sense of smell, which they use to track people like Spidey uses his spider-sense.

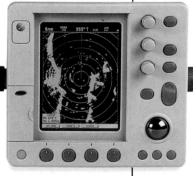

Radar
Ships and airplanes use radar [RAY-dar] to follow things moving nearby. The other objects show up as dots on the radar screen.

Spider-Man also uses his spider-sense to track his enemies. Peter Parker has created a special device called a "spider-tracker." It is specially tuned in to Spider-Man's spider-sense. When the tracker is placed on a person or a vehicle, Spider-Man can track it no matter where it goes.

For instance, if Spider-Man wants to find out where the Kingpin's hideout is, he can place a spider-tracker on one of the bad guy's cars. Then, without being seen, Spidey can follow the car using spider-sense.

Whether ducking flying objects, or tracking suspects, Spider-Man uses spider-sense like a ship uses radar to "see" what is ahead. Spidey would still be powerful without spider-sense...but he'd probably have a few more bruises.

Shhh! Don't tell!

Whether as Peter Parker or Spider-Man, Spidey usually places his spider-trackers on people or things secretly. If they know that he is following them, they might simply destroy the tracking device.

Tiny tracker

The spider-tracker itself (in circle) is shaped like a spider. Made of very lightweight metals and plastic, the device can stick to any surface. It sends out signals that only Spidey's spider-sense can track.

Shhh!
Very few people know Spider-Man's secret identity. One villain who found out was the Green Goblin (below), who attacked Peter's family.

Peter's powers

Under Spidey's mask and skintight costume is a regular guy named Peter Parker. Peter has to use all his natural knowledge and ability to operate as the great Spider-Man.

Those webs he shoots don't come out of his arms. *Someone* had to invent Spidey's secret web fluid.

When his costume gets ripped by the slashing claws of a villain, someone has to sew it up.

And Spider-Man can't just eat insects like real spiders. Someone has to earn money to buy food, just like everyone else.

That someone is Peter Parker. Peter uses his great knowledge of chemistry and science to keep Spider-Man's gear on the cutting edge. He mixes the secret

web formula to ensure that Spidey always has a web to swing on. He uses his knowledge of science to solve some of the mysteries Spider-Man encounters. Once, he used liquid oxygen to freeze a bomb that had been strapped to his wrist.

Spider lunch
Spider-Man eats regular food, but real spiders enjoy munching on insects such as flies. Some types of spiders, such as tarantulas, eat small animals.

Sew what?
Super heroes don't all have assistants to take care of their gear. Here Spider-Man uses needle and thread to fix his ripped costume.

An eye on Spidey
Peter uses a remote control camera to take pictures of Spider-Man. Remote control means that it can be operated from a distance.

Spider hater
J. Jonah Jameson is the publisher of the *Daily Bugle*. He thinks Spider-Man is a danger to the community.

To earn money to have a place to live and to keep his spider-body strong, Peter works as a photographer for a newspaper called the *Daily Bugle*. He uses a remote-control camera to take pictures of himself in action and then sells the photos. Somehow, the publisher of the *Bugle*, the loudmouthed J. Jonah Jameson, has never figured out how Peter always seems to know where Spider-Man is.

In recent years, Peter also has taken a job as a research scientist, using his chemistry education to learn more about science...and to earn a living.

Peter also is the source of Spider-Man's great interest in helping people. Not everyone thinks Spider-Man is a good guy, and he often has to avoid the police to do his work. Peter helps keep Spider-Man focused on the job at hand.

For all of his great abilities to swing from webs, stick to walls, or wrestle huge villains, Peter Parker knows that Spider-Man's greatest power is his ability to help people.

Spider-Man learned long ago that with great power comes great responsibility. Peter's ability to understand —and live up to—that ideal is what really turns Spider-Man from a spider-powered guy into a super hero. Learning that lesson can turn you into a super hero, too.

Peter must be ready to spring into action at all times, as Spidey or as a photographer.

Looking for answers
Research scientists work in all kinds of fields, looking for answers to scientific mysteries and solving problems using science.

Man on the go
The life of a photographer keeps Peter as busy as his work as Spider-Man. Peter's main challenge is learning to balance these two busy parts of his life.

Glossary

Abdomen
In spiders, the second, or hindmost, of two main body parts; it contains the organs that help it spin webs.

Agility
Being nimble, quick, and able to move speedily in any direction.

Arachnid
[uh-RACK-nid]
The scientific name for the type of creature that spiders are. Just as all dogs and humans are mammals, all spiders are arachnids.

Ballooning
A type of spider behavior in which young spiders shoot out several strands of webbing and use them somewhat like parachutes to glide short distances through the air.

Barbell
Used by weightlifters, a barbell is made of a long iron bar with disks of iron hung near each end. More disks can be added to make the barbell heavier.

Cartridge [KAR-trij]
A small, sealed case that is placed within a larger machine or object. In Spider-Man's case, he uses cartridges of web fluid in his web-shooters.

Cephalothorax
[seh-FAL-oh-THOR-ax]
The first of the two main body parts of a spider. The mouth and sense organs are here.

DNA
A chemical that is found in every human cell. DNA tells cells how to grow and what body parts they should become. DNA stands for "deoxy-ribonucleic acid."

ESP
Initials for "extra-sensory perception." Some people believe that those with powerful minds can read the thoughts of others, can predict the future, and can move objects using brainpower alone.

Gravity
The physical force that binds together objects on earth and in space. Gravity keeps the earth spinning around the sun, and keeps everything on earth from flying off into space.

Mimic
Another word for imitate; to re-create or copy someone or something.

Proportionate
[pro-PORSH-en-uht]
The relationship of one thing to another, sometimes different,

thing. For instance, Peter Parker has the proportionate strength of a spider.

Radar
A type of electronic device that can show and track distant objects, such as planes or ships.

Radioactivity
Many living things and minerals send out different types of waves of energy. These waves are measured as radioactivity.

Research
The process of studying a subject with the goal of learning more about it than is known right now.

Venom
Poisonous liquid put out by the bites of some spiders and snakes.

Vibrations
The sounds, energy, or waves put out when something moves rapidly back and forth.

Web
The constructions weaved by spiders using silky threads that they shoot out of special organs on their bodies.

Index

PROFICIENT **4** READER

$3.95

Web-slinging, wall-crawling, spider-sense, and more. Read about the awesome powers of Spider-Man!

DORLING KINDERSLEY *READERS*

Stunning photographs combine with lively illustrations and engaging, age-appropriate stories in DORLING KINDERSLEY *READERS*, a multilevel reading program guaranteed to capture children's interest while developing their reading skills and general knowledge.

BEGINNING **1** TO READ	Beginning to read	• Word repetition, limited vocabulary, and simple sentences • Picture dictionary boxes
BEGINNING **2** TO READ ALONE	Beginning to read alone	• Longer sentences and increased vocabulary • Information boxes full of extra fun facts
READING **3** ALONE	Reading alone	• More complex sentence structure • Information boxes and alphabetical glossary
PROFICIENT **4** READERS	Proficient readers	• Rich vocabulary and challenging sentence structure • Additional information and alphabetical glossary

With Dorling Kindersley Readers, children will learn to read – then read to learn!

ISBN 0-7894-7923-0

M8098-I/IN
53

see our complete catalog at
www.dk.com

Printed in China

9000

9 780789 479235

6.2/1.0